Written by Fred Walker
Photography by Joe Worsley

sundance™
A Haights Cross Communications Company

Everywhere I look, I see lines.

Lines of sunshine fall on my deck. Even the deck has lines.

Sometimes I try to count all the lines I see, but there are way too many lines.

Our next-door neighbors have a whole fence full of lines!

Lines make beautiful windows and doors.
Some lines are straight. Some lines are curved.

This whole house is lines!
When the house is done it will
still have lines . . . of bricks and
windows and doors.

Lines on streets help drivers know which way to go.

And parking lot lines show them where to park when they get there.

When I get to school, I find even more lines.

People stand in lines for lots of reasons . . . to get a drink of water . . . and to get lunch.

Nature makes lines, too . . .
I spot lines of weeds standing in
the sun.

Lightning is a crinkly line that
looks like a rip in the sky. . . .
I wonder what kind of line
thunder would make.

Do you see the lines in the bark
of this tree?
These lines are very, very,
VERY squiggly lines.
But they are still lines.

Most lines in nature are squiggly.
Trees and flowers can grow in
straight lines.
But only when people plant them
that way.

I look for lines because they are very important.

It would be hard to play football . . . or hopscotch, or even pickup sticks . . . without any lines.

And without lines, we wouldn't have any hair to comb!

I like the lines that make music . . .
lines of strings or a line of keys
sitting side by side.

But before I say any more about lines, it's time for my favorite dinner.